TELL ME A STORY, DAD

Retold by Virginia Ferguson and Peter Durkin
Illustrated by Mitch Vane

"Tell me a story, Dad!"

"What kind of story?"

"An animal story. I like animals."

LITTLE RED RIDING HOOD

"What kind of animal?"

"A wild animal that lives in the forest, has sharp teeth, and howls at night. A wolf."

"Are there any people in the story?"

"Yes. I want an old lady who lives
by herself in the forest.
And a woodcutter.
And a little girl."

"What happens? Is it a dangerous story?"

"Yes. It is dangerous—in the forest.
The wolf finds out
where the little girl is going,
and races on ahead
to the old lady's house."

"What happens when the little girl arrives at the house?"

"She goes inside,
and is surprised to see how big
Grandma's ears and eyes and teeth are."

"Don't tell me the wolf had dressed up in the grandma's nightie?"

"Yes, that's right. He ate her up and then dressed up in her nightie."

“This is a sad sort of story.
I don’t like the idea of a decent
grandmother inside a wolf.”

“Oh, it’s all right.
The little girl screams,
and a woodcutter rushes in
and chops the wolf open.
Grandma pops out, quite safe,
and the little girl is taken home safely.”

LITTLE RED RIDING HOO

"By the way, what was she wearing?"

"I forgot to say—a little red riding hood.
That was a great story, Dad.
Could I have another one?"

"No, not tonight. I'm tired out
after all that storytelling.
Maybe tomorrow night –
I'll have some more ideas by then."